The Wicked Flowers
of Charles Baudelaire

THE WICKED FLOWERS
OF CHARLES BAUDELAIRE

A Selection
Limericked by

Jan Owen

Shoestring Press

All rights reserved. No part of this work covered by the copyright herein may be reproduced or used in any means – graphic, electronic, or mechanical, including copying, recording, taping, or information storage and retrieval systems – without written permission of the publisher.

Printed by imprintdigital
Upton Pyne, Exeter
www.imprintdigital.com

Typesetting and cover design by narrator
www.narrator.me.uk
info@narrator.me.uk
033 022 300 39

Published by Shoestring Press
19 Devonshire Avenue, Beeston, Nottingham, NG9 1BS
(0115) 925 1827
www.shoestringpress.co.uk

First published 2016
© Copyright: Jan Owen

The moral right of the author has been asserted.

Cover image: 'Poppies' by Katsushika Hokusai

ISBN 978-1-910323-60-1

ACKNOWLEDGEMENTS

My gratitude to the incomparable Charles Baudelaire for his masterwork *Les Fleurs du Mal*, and my apologies for this descent from the sublime to the ridiculous.

I am grateful to Arts South Australia for a 2015 grant which enabled me to finish several projects including this collection.

For Tony

CONTENTS

To the Reader	1
BILE AND BEYOND	3
PARIS	29
WINOS	35
WICKED FLOWERS	39
REVOLTING	43
CLOSING TIME	47
ODDS AND SODS	51
NOTES	57
Afterword	63

TO THE READER

Dear hypocrite reader, my twin,
I'm damned if we have to begin
  With Spleen and Disease,
  Necrophilia, Sleaze…
Quel ennui! Let's invent a *new* sin.

Bile and Beyond

BENEDICTION

One rises above family spite
When promised a crown of Pure Light:
The poet's main Duty
Is suffering for Beauty.
Maman asserts that's Pure Shite.

THE ALBATROSS

We poets seem gauche half the time
Like an albatross trapped in its prime
But caught in full flight
Down the pub Friday night,
Full of beer, we are bloody sublime.

ELEVATION

What they slip you in Saint-Germain bars
Could put you in orbit round Mars
But I shall get high
On the vast azure sky
In a time capsule aimed at the stars.

I LOVE IMAGINING THOSE NAKED DAYS

Time was we were classically slim
And rollicking nude on a whim
Was quite *comme il faut*.
Now we're flabby as dough,
Allons-y, ma chérie, to the gym!

CORRESPONDENCES

Your skull is a cool mixing bowl
Of colour, scent, music and soul.
Plop symbolic gloop
In your Swedenborg soup
And serve with cold pilsner. Skol!

THE SICK MUSE

You're a misery this morning, my dear;
Quit the brandy and wipe off that sneer.
You're malingering in spite,
Spewing verses so trite
My critics won't snigger, they'll jeer.

THE JINX

You can sod the Academy game,
If I can't have some modest acclaim
I'll retire to Mauritius,
Unfuckingambitious,
And write filthy limericks on fame.

BEAUTY

I'm Medusa with sexier eyes –
Poets dub me the Sphinx of the Skies.
Quite a balancing act
When you're noseless and cracked.
Don't stand underneath if you're wise.

DON JUAN IN HELL

As he crosses the Styx they gasp 'Yes'
But he scorns to respond; it's my guess
He's a sexual wreck
With an arthritic neck
Only hoping that Charon plays chess.

THE GIANTESS

I feel like some pussy in clover
Snuggled up to her white cliffs of Dover.
It's the Late Pleistocene,
I'm her cat, she's my queen.
Mon Dieu – she's about to roll over!

JEWELS

She was naked and – knowing my thing –
Bespangled and jingling with bling.
As the fire flared and died
So did we (and I cried).
The first time since early last spring.

EXOTIC PERFUME

I'm dreaming of tropical shores
And very nude nudes with pawpaws –
I'm getting high, Pet,
On the tides of your sweat
And the surf-crashing swell of your snores.

YOUR HAIR

So you've put a blue rinse through your hair
Which smells of sardines. I don't care,
It's a sea of delight
I've been swimming all night –
I'm exhausted, please tell me I'm there.

I WORSHIP YOU

My adored, I keep losing my grip;
Stop wriggling around or I'll slip.
We're so un-X-rated
I'm hyperfrustrated!
Let's get out the handcuffs and whip.

YOU'D TAKE THE UNIVERSE TO BED

Why haul the whole world into bed
When you could have had *moi*, Charles, instead?
I flatly refuse
A slut for a Muse –
I'm a genius already – drop dead!

UNSATISFIED

You've made this bed hell. It's unchic
To keep pleading. I'm off for a leak.
And put that cigar
Straight back in the jar,
You've set fire to the sheets twice this week.

YOUR SLINKY GOWN

Green satin and sequins enhance
Your serpentine sway, your cold glance.
My angel, my Sphinx,
My snake-charming minx,
Your cobra's got into my pants.

A CARCASS

Quoting Poe, I tried squeezing her bust
While she whined at the heat and the dust.
She fainted of course
When we passed the dead horse
And I held forth on maggots and lust.

DE PROFUNDIS CLAMAVI

My nose is alarmingly runny,
I'm hoarse, I can't write, I've no money,
I cough, my feet hurt,
I need a clean shirt…
Come at once, bringing lemons and honey!

THE VAMPIRE

Bloody bitch, though I might have put paid
To you once and for all with a spade
Or a cyanide pill,
At the thought of you ill
I learned CPR and First Aid.

COME, MY SWEET CAT

You've the perfumed electrical fur
Of my woman, sweet puss. Plus you purr.
You've the same spiky gaze!
This is no passing phase –
I vastly prefer you to her.

THE BALCONY

Remember, dear heart, the rose mist
And the hiccups I got when we kissed?
I forget what we said,
I was hopeless in bed,
But of course we were both of us pissed.

A GHOST

Your beauty once drove me ecstatic;
Now your mirror's been stashed in the attic.
 So what's for my dinner,
 You spooky old sinner?
(We're cosy now, not acrobatic.)

I GIVE YOU THESE LINES

I'll be famous one day, wait and see!
Then what are *you* likely to be?
 A maddening refrain
 In the stunned reader's brain
Since everyone hates you but me.

THE WAY IT IS

I don't want to chat and that's flat–
And stop mussing up my cravat.
Tell me beautiful lies,
Let me drown in your eyes. . .
I habitually do with my cat.

ALL OF HER

It's her whole soulful self I adore
But the Devil keeps asking for more.
D'accord: a neat bum,
Cute twat, tits and tum,
And a vicious tongue. How do I score?

THE SPIRITUAL DAWN

While deeply engaged with Céline
I was thinking of you, my chaste queen.
Which spoilt the whole night
And I left at first light
So do let us wipe the sheet clean.

TO ONE WHO IS TOO JOYOUS

You're so happy, I wish you were dead,
Just lying there, hogging the bed.
Quite frankly, I'm lusting
For acts so disgusting
I'd better just write them instead.

EVENING HARMONY

Pink perfume and blossom and skin
And the sob of a pink violin:
I feel in the pink,
It's the sunset, I think,
And this very pink glass of pink gin.

THE PERFUME BOTTLE

They can smell us from here to the Loire
For the fusty old things that we are.
I've told you so often,
Get back in your coffin
Or splash on some *Eau de Lazare*!

POISON

Forget hash and wine – for pure dread
Check out her saliva instead.
In fact I should add
Her breath is so bad
Last night I fell clean out of bed.

CLOUDY SKY

You remind me of wet winter days
And the backdrops of second-rate plays –
I love and abhor you,
Detest and adore you.
It's probably just a brief craze.

THE CAT IN MY HEAD

There's a cat walking round in my brain,
Six flamingos, two skunks, a Great Dane
    And an unhousetrained gnu.
    Holy cow, call the zoo
Before the smell drives me insane.

THE BEAUTIFUL SHIP

Maman says you're putting on weight.
Like a tramp steamer taking on freight,
    With a strong whiff of brine
    Sub-Plimsoll line.
How's that as a pitch for a date?

INVITATION TO THE VOYAGE

Let's head to some misty Dutch place
And screw till we're blue in the face.
The ticket's my shout;
If it doesn't work out…
Sis, give us a fiver, in case.

A LITTLE CHAT

Though you stroke my poor bosom in vain,
That dogsmeat, that palace, that pain
Feels quite a bit better for
This muddled metaphor…
(Maybe I'll start this again.)

AUTUMN SONG

With winter next week the time's ripe
For my poetic licence to gripe.
(If you make a profession
Of seasonal depression
It sucks in the motherly type.)

SADNESS AND WANDERING

Matron, Agatha's shot through again,
Shall I check out the 10.15 train?
Last seen? By the green
With a porn magazine
And a Baedeker guidebook on Spain.

CATS

O that sensuous, powerful grace,
Those glinting eyes vacant as space!
Dear Pussy my liege
You've the *noblesse oblige*
Of a vastly superior race.

OWLS

These insufferable avian prigs
Who've chosen my yew for their digs
Perch morning to night
Disapproving of light.
I hope they all fall off their twigs.

MUSIC

It's a sea for the timid and nervy;
You're safe as you dip, topsy-turvy.
Such joy! Such ennui!
I'm the tall ship for me –
No seasickness, danger, or scurvy.

THE CRACKED BELL

If I said I could sing I'd be lying.
I am. In a pool of blood, dying
By corpses piled high,
God only knows why,
But one ought to be sanguine. I'm trying.

SPLEEN: MEMORIES

My memory's a tomb on display –
Do regard the remains of the day.
   I've got worms up the butt
   And the pharmacy's shut…
I forget what I wanted to say.

SPLEEN: KING OF A PLUVIOUS LAND

No absinthe, it's raining again
And we've just had a burst water main
   But never mind that
   I've at last cracked a fat
Which is hard down a stormwater drain.

SPLEEN: THE LONG LOW SKY

I've a lousy hand – Théo is dealing –
And the sky's coming in through the ceiling.
There are spiders, the bat
On the lampshade just shat,
It's a bad trip, don't ask how we're feeling.

THE TASTE OF NOTHINGNESS

Hay fever, hey ring-a-ding-ding,
So much for the perfumes of Spring.
I'm knackered. Time flies.
For a fitting demise
An avalanche might be the thing.

THE SELF-TORTURER

I belt you about in fine style
And your only response is a smile!
If you don't bloody cry
I shall suck my heart dry
(Though my usual tipple's black bile).

THE CLOCK

Count the Tics and the Tocs of cruel Fate
(Arithmetic's easy to hate)
And you'll find to have Fun
Then repent what you've Done
It is always already Too Late.

Paris

THE SWAN

Andromache, where have you gone?
What has Mallarmé done with my Swan?
Damn the new Carrousel,
This town's gone to hell!
Frank Villon's best line is spot on.

SEVEN OLD MEN

A line of them, lame and half-blind,
Lurches by – am I losing my mind?
Must be the DTs.
I've gone weak at the knees
So I might as well tag on behind.

LITTLE OLD WOMEN

As the dolly birds all get away
I've been stalking old biddies since May
With compassionate glee
That it's them and not me
Dead certain to croak any day.

TO A WOMAN PASSING BY

We're swanning along Quai Voltaire:
She's gorgeous and I'm debonair.
As we pass, our eyes meet
And I'm swept off my feet…
Dogshit again. It's not fair.

THE DIGGING SKELETON

I was hoping for heavenly bliss
Till some *poète maudit* took the piss.
  Though I'd rather be *sotto*,
  Keep Smiling's my motto.
(Arthritis had nothing on this!)

GAMBLING

Old poets and their tarts on a spree:
  How *poncif*. I went for a pee
  Then woke from the dream,
  Caught in midstream,
And felt terribly sorry for me.

I HAVE NOT FORGOTTEN

Our little white house, your distress
That my bedroom was always a mess
As I scribbled my verses
On humping in hearses,
In Latin so you'd never guess.

Winos

THE RAGPICKERS' WINE

Down this alley each night around ten
Weaves Bonaparte leading his men
To honour and glory.
The end of the story –
Dead drunk in the gutter again.

THE MURDERER'S WINE

I've bundled my wife down the well.
She was asking for it, was my Nell.
Now I'm free, I can booze
And bang who I choose!
For a caring bloke, marriage is hell.

THE WINE OF THE LONER

Some spare cash for sex would be nice
And Adeline might at half-price.
But my bottle of wine
As a Muse is divine
And it's cheaper and won't give me lice.

THE LOVERS' WINE

Sister mine, we're both under the weather.
Here we come, Paradise, hell for leather!
Let's gallop, swim, fly
Through the crystal-clear sky.
How ecstatic to vomit together!

Wicked Flowers

A MARTYRED WOMAN

This was more than your ordinary fling:
Her head was propped up by the Ming
In rather bad form –
A ranunculus corm.
We're not planting bulbs for the spring.

DAMNED WOMEN:
DELPHINE AND HIPPOLYTE

While they're languidly taking a spell
Hippolyte starts to moan about hell.
(Here, I threw in some tropes
About slippery slopes
But the Censor condemned me as well.)

THE FOUNTAIN OF BLOOD

My Valentine gift from that whore
Was a fresh bed of nails. *Merde alors*,
　　These metaphors stink –
　　I should get to a shrink
Before you all drown in my gore.

VOYAGE TO CYTHERA

It's pitched to the honeymoon set
But the gallows make newly-weds fret
　　And the corpse with no nuts
　　Disgorging its guts
Is not picturesque. Try Tibet.

Revolting

THE REBEL

An angel swoops down on his prey,
'Learn some charity, wretch, while you may!'
'God help me, I won't!'
'I'll be damned if you don't!'
So now there's the devil to pay.

THE DENIAL OF SAINT PETER

Since lopping off ears is a crime,
I'd have chickened out too at the time.
A shame. All the same,
It's the rooster I blame.
Such a cock-up I'm stuck for a rhyme.

ABEL AND CAIN

A family business is tricky:
The Boss knows you're faking that sickie.
And when you're downvoted
While Bro is promoted
In general the outcome is sticky.

LITANIES TO SATAN

We'd best give the Devil his due
While warming our safe Sunday pew.
Two bob each way
With today's state of play
Pascal would've hedged his bets too.

Closing Time

THE DEATH OF THE LOVERS

La petite mort palls, I confess;
We could go for the big time, I guess.
Do you know what I'd like?
A joint lightning strike
Then an angel to clear up the mess.

THE DEATH OF THE POOR

Divine dreams are all very well
But a good poker hand would be swell.
And as a reward
For our meekness, dear Lord,
Pitch every rich bastard to Hell.

THE DEATH OF ARTISTS

I'm a sculptor in plaster and wire.
The critics suggest I aim higher.
 Well I don't give a sod
 For the Glory of God,
He can do it Himself, I retire.

TRAVELLING

Sea trips are not healthy for chaps,
They're a series of frightful mishaps.
 Bon voyage, Maxime,
 I've settled for dream:
I'm the Left Bank flâneur of old maps.

Odds and Sods

THE LID

Haute cuisine: the Almighty cooks well –
A fine bouillabaisse, by the smell.
We're all in the pot
Which is getting too hot
And they're licking their lips down in Hell.

THE VOICE

There were two of them, both on the make
With their offers of all I could take –
Either gateaux or dreams:
I'm schizo it seems.
(If you ever hear voices, choose cake.)

THE ABYSS

Blaise is dreary and God is a grump;
His infinity gives me the hump.
There are holes in my dreams,
Maths is worse than it seems,
Life's a bugger, I might as well jump.

THE COMPLAINT OF AN ICARUS

Pour la gloire de la France it was done,
Plus I wanted my day in the sun.
Five miles in free fall
Was an absolute ball.
Now the parachute's failed, it's less fun.

MEDITATION

It's my creditors. Thy will be dun.
(This is no time to try a weak pun!)
I shall lurk in the Parc
Monceau till it's dark
Then give them the finger and run.

EPIGRAPH FOR A CONDEMNED BOOK

Best read without casting aspersions
On blasphemy, drugs and perversions.
And if you're not chuffed
You can go and get stuffed:
Be damned if I'll write you clean versions.

Notes

DESPATCH TO GENERAL AUPICK

You claim that my youth was misspent.
Bien sûr, it's my artistic bent –
I'm of no fixed abode,
A flâneur of the road,
Since posterity won't pay the rent.

LETTER TO MME AUPICK

Ma mère, I must seem an ingrate
To be thanking you seven months late.
And now, what a bore,
I need more. *Je t'implore!*
Five hundred at least – it won't wait.

NOTE TO NADAR

Come at 4 p.m., Felix, my dear:
My likeness could make your career.
I propose a Poe pose
(But downplay my nose).
Re the fee: could we settle next year?

RUMINATION

An obsession with fame is a curse.
You'll agree only envy ranks worse.
Shall I summon the nerve
To beseech Uncle Beuve
For some niggardly praise of my verse?

TO THE CHIEF CENSOR

Monsieur, you have made me your debtor:
By ignoring both spirit and letter,
You cretinous tort,
You disgrace to the court,
You have spurred me to write even better.

APOLOGY TO POULET-MALASSIS

I've spent your advance, my dear brother,
But sold the poems on to another.
Forgive me, dear Chook,
One must think of the Book.
Don't breathe a word to my mother.

AFTERWORD

Even a loser can win:
You too could put a new spin
On the wicked, the mad,
The bad sex you've had,
Hash, sacrilege, VD and gin.